ADVANCED PRAISE

I am awed by her depth of feeling, awareness of beauty, and ability to know and see beneath the surface of life.
— Robin Easton: Author, *Naked in Eden*

The title poem, "Lowly Listening", is filled with imagery and allusions to a message we will collectively never forget; imagery of such eloquence that her words stretch far beyond the ones we so often seek as wordsmiths.
— Dan Kelly: Journalist

I hear the sea, walk the marshlands, and witness the changing seasons in these poems of deep devotion to nature and Zen. With strength and contrast, they are light-inspired, filled with the beauty of musicality and, most of all, profoundly moving.
—Kate Lamberg: Long Island Beat Poet Emerita

"Come Lie With Me" is a most beautiful poem that deeply affects my heart and soul. I continue to read it over and over again and find solace in its powerful peace.
—Art Edson: Nature Photographer

It is a profound experience to accompany her on walks with 'air filled with ocean' and listen to her songs of transformation, so masterfully painted with words. One by one she opens the petals of her heart's wisdom and dives into its very center of joy.
—Heloise Idstein: Poet

She has a way of weaving reflections of beauty, and beauty of her own generating, with words that outperform any construct of my imagination, both deep and filled with light.
—Mary Ann Van Leeuwen: Nature Photographer

As in a seamless eye-flow of sandpipers across the ocean, these poems gently carry me to a specific point — at once indescribable and yet deeply familiar.
— Rich Vancouver, Nature Photographer

I have shared these poems with friends as gifts of words clothed in poignant human experience. Her writing is so clear, and yet part of what can only be called the Mysterious Beautiful.
—Susan Debra Hall-West: Poet

"Endurance", with its beautiful feminine images, literally takes my breath away.
—Elaine Mansfield: Award-winning independent author, *Leaning into Love: A Spiritual Journey Through Grief*

Plain Perfect! Her poems in honor of Native Americans carry a spiritual weight like soft winter winds across the western plains, with words and visuals so strong and rich in texture that they pierce my soul with authenticity.
—Kate Bostrom: Owner, A Balanced Horse

I'm deeply grateful for these poems in honor of Native Americans and that her light is shining during my lifetime.
—Linda Collins-Thomas: Author and Playwright who teaches at the Osher Institute at the University of Rhode Island

Her talent is a miraculous gift, and one she delivers straight to our hearts in "Land Beautiful Beyond Description".
—Sandy Frantz-Rademaker: retired Professor of French Literature at Aquinas College

LOWLY LISTENING

POEMS FROM THE FARM COAST

SARAH RAGSDALE

Published by Rudd Rambles Press
www.ruddrambles.com

Lowly Listening © Sarah Ragsdale
Front Cover Farm Coast Photo © Christine Chitnis
Press Logo and Cover Design: Sarah Kate Ragsdale

All Rights Reserved.

"Lowly Listening" is a phrase from Ralph Waldo Emerson's *Essays: First Series*, "Spiritual Laws". Throughout this book are fragments from Emerson's talks, poems from Rumi and Hafiz, whom he admired, and Hindu's sacred text, The Upanishads, which inspired him. Also included are fragments from Dōgen, a Zen Buddhist monk and poet, and Kabir, an Indian mystic poet.

The following poems were previously published. *Pathfinder Magazine:* "Come, Lie With Me", "Talking To Myself In The Night" (titled "Soul's Longing for Itself"), "Ocean of Wisdom (titled "I Once Leapt"). *Wickford Poetry & Art:* "Lowly Listening", "The Old Vintner's Daughter", "for Land Beautiful Beyond Description, "Under The Moon Of Falling Leaves", part of the permanent collection of contemporary poetry at Poet's House in New York City.

FIRST EDITION

ISBN 978-0-578-38353-8
Printed in the United States of America

Library in Congress Cataloging-in-Publication Data
Ragsdale, Sarah
Title: Lowly Listening: Poems From The Farm Coast
Identifiers: LCCN 202390597
Nature Poetry | Emerson | Buddhism | Native Americans

To the loves of my life ~

My children and their partners,
Sarah Kate & Anthony and Benjamin & Stephanie;
my grandchildren, Eli and Avery; my husband, Mark;
and in memory of my parents

CONTENTS

While these poems invite browsing, reading them in sequence may be more meaningful. As in a spiritual journey, poems of mindfulness are followed by poems of impermanence which, when fully accepted, can change our fixed ideas about everything, including ourselves. By accepting the instability and preciousness of all life, we move into a transformative way of perceiving and being, with poems that celebrate a loosening of attachments and an intimacy with life's inherent joy. The final poems honor our legacy of Native Americans, including the Sakonnet Tribe of southeastern New England's Farm Coast, the Sioux at Standing Rock, and the Hopi at Third Mesa.

Come Lie With Me	5
Signs	6
All Is Rust and Stardust	7
Migration	8
Sound of No Sound	9
On Allens Pond	10
Twilight Fun and Frivolity	12
An Illumination	14
Full Moon Eclipse	15
One Moon	16
Merging Metaphysics	17
Sky	18
Lowly Listening	21
You Remember Too	23
Shadows	24
The First Winter of My Grief	25
A Blue Winter Forest	26
Twilight Jewel of the Forest Wisdom	27
An Opportunity	28
The Weaver	30
Musings under the Snow Sky	31
Spring Is Coming, I Know	32
Perigee Tide	35

Blackberry Spring	36
The Big Thaw	37
Band of Burros	38
A Living Sanctuary	39
In the Night Garden	40
Talking to Myself in the Night	42
Lying Down upon the Green	44
Elephant Rock	47
Beach Walk Surprise	48
Ocean of Wisdom	49
The Dance	50
Sandpipers	52
The Other Shore	53
On Stellwagen Bank	54
Summer Sunset	56
Black Swallowtail	57
Red-Winged Blackbird	58
Amrita in the Garden	59
The Old Vintner's Daughter	63
Their Old-Fashioned Tango	65
Everything Tastes Better with Lemons	66
One Last Cup of Love	67
Already Broken	68
The Shell Seeker	69
Her Ladies Desk	70
Little Blue Kisses	72
Under the Moon of Falling Leaves	78
Soul Remembering	82
For Land Beautiful beyond Description	83
Resilience	85
Old Orabi	88

Glossary
Note: Lowly Listening
Acknowledgments
About the Author
About the Press

*There is dew on these poems in the morning and
at night a cool breeze may rise from them.*

*In the winter they are blankets,
in the summer a place to swim.*

— KABIR

fall

Every natural fact is a symbol of some spiritual fact.

— **EMERSON** | Nature

Come Lie With Me

Born in the dying season
of umbers and vermillion
juniper berries and frost

Come, lie with me, in the deer beds

We'll nestle into their quiet whorls
of sun-bleached grasses that grow
close to the edge of the sea

Come, lie with me, in the deer beds

We'll warm our bodies beside
the rising tendrils of heat smoke
from soft wildness

Come, lie with me, in the deer beds

We'll waken to the whoosh
of wings taking flight from
these sacred earth mandalas

Come, lie with me, in the deer beds

Signs

Flash of yellow
leaf or goldfinch?

the old red barn
bathed in light
through thinning trees

All Is Rust and Stardust

Beneath the washed blue-violet sky
the weathered door in our garden wall
is covered with many layers

of faded teal   burnt umber   hints of white

Its peeling paint and rusty hinges
a gentle reminder nothing lasts,
only impermanence

Migration

purple bellied clouds droop
o'er wild mustard meadows
bent with soft brush strokes of
wings leaving

Sound of No Sound

When sounds of geese migrating break
the silence of a late afternoon un the garden
the whole world falls silent —

Suddenly enters the spaciousness
of No-Being and No Non-Being *

Suddenly enters the silence following
the first sound of the Great Bell —

the call of Buddha
for all living beings to hear it clearly
so that all suffering in them may cease

* *Glossary*

Allens Pond

The sky is overcast and the air
filled with ocean on my afternoon walk
to see the last of Fall's colors —

beyond a well-kept stonewall
tracing the farmer's fallow field
blue-black elderberries stand laced
with orange and yellow bittersweet
breaking open

dove-gray bayberries
speckled like flecked eggs
entwine in nests with rose hips
faded from first frost

At the end of the path lies a hard-scrabble beach
where I'm not expecting to see anything more

but then —

A bright yellow cinquefoil
rising from rubble!

The cragged branch on an old scrub pine
pointing towards the sky —

Nature's Finger Pointing Toward the Moon*

*Glossary

Twilight Fun and Frivolity

Beneath the shadows of sienna scrub oaks

electric-pink haired marsh maidens

dance to the tunes of chappy blue fiddlers

sway to the sea shanties of tear-striped kestrels

before drifting off to sleep on the incoming tide

nestled in beds of blossomed white cotton

If the stars should appear but one night every thousand years how man would marvel and stare.

— EMERSON | Nature

An Illumination

A shooting star streaks
across the midnight sky
giving birth to an illumination —

the eternal image of a child
building sandcastles by the sea,
as Libra's occidental lyre plays on

A single blaze of light
taking measure
of the tides of our lives

Full Moon Eclipse

As the moon
filled with fires of countless
sunrises and sunsets

floats across the midnight sky
to embrace her lover
shadows our light

a flurry of bird calls
followed by mournful cries
of coyotes calling howling yipping —

too far to see
wedding--white moonflowers
piercing the 'shadow of abandonment' *

*From the Greek, *Ekleípō*

One Moon

Half-moon Full moon
Bright moon Blue moon

Zen likes to reminds us
there is only One Moon,
always full and complete

Merging Metaphysics

Many live their whole lives wondering
about the meaning of existence

Heraclitus and Parmenides debated:
Do all things flow like a river and nothing abides
or does nothing ever change, it only seems to?

Hegel believed both to be true but then
I had my own experience with death
that I will never forget —

the unchanging, unified field of Parmenides
the ancient rishis of the Upanishads, yes

and yet, and yet . . .

as Rumi might further say,
to describe the feeling behind this experience,
a Sentient Field of Love

Sky

Sky in Puddle
Window to Eternity

winter

*We must be willing to place ourselves
full center in our lives in order to receive
the revelations that await us, by Lowly Listening.*

— **EMERSON** | Nature Lectures

Lowly Listening

The wind is hard-swept as I set out to clear the cobwebs
from too long inside a winter's day

I hope to capture the sun's late slant on the deserted beach
but when I see someone in the distance
it isn't hard to recognize another version of my solitary self

or how the fading light shadows our footprints
turns the colors of wet sand into a carpet of pink crystalline
blackens breaches of rocks with snow still caught in their crevices

yet it is the fierce surf that commands my attention . . .
its rising and plummeting plumes filling the sky
with a purple-hued grit —

mineral - laced oysters broken shards of sea

glass briny shrimp from distant shores

towers of smoke rising and falling

squids' indigo ink scribbling final messages

upon collapsing walls

and in the resounding roars
of life falling backwards upon itself
a silence born of sound

the sight of a lone, pale gray winged gull
standing still on shaly rock

lowly listening

Author's Note

Permanent collection of contemporary poetry at Poets House, NYC

You Remember Too

I woke to December's hoary grass
tattered with its remnants
of summer's green —

the phone call came later in the day,
the one with silence on the other end

You remember, too,
the year Christmas was not Merry
but Bright with Wings.

Shadows
(haiku)

three low-flying hawks
small birds seeking quick refuge
bare thorny privet

The First Winter of My Grief

I watch an early morning light
reach into the lower boughs
of the garden's hemlocks,
to warm small sleeping birds

Satisfied, she moves behind
distant hardwoods,
to cast long shadows across
wide fields of bleached wheat

A Blue Winter Forest

When I can't sleep I like to imagine
I am in a blue winter forest standing
on the rim of a deep canyon with
a silver river running through it —

at my feet is a ladder of coarse hemp
I grab hold of, climb halfway down
to a cave where a crackling fire awaits

reach for my heavy woolen cloak kept
on a wooden peg, wrap it around my
shoulders to sit and watch the firelight

caress the charcoaled flanks of bison
and reindeer running across rough rock
when out of the darkness a baby goat emerges

nestles into my arms and as I hold her close
stroke her soft wild body, I feel at peace

Jewel of the Forest Wisdom *

Snow-capped feeders sway
under the weight of cardinals
and other birds

a scurry of squirrels
skulks slippery stonewalls
wary of their welcome —

only the old oak is standing still

draped in her mala beads of iced dew
Moon reflected in every dewdrop *

* *Glossary*

An Opportunity

Prepared or not death comes —

it is the ones left behind
who have an opportunity to love
in ways we and they cannot yet imagine,
as life strips away our differences

Lift the veil of your heart.
Only the words of the wise will remain.
The weaver, getting good or bad yarn
and connecting karmas with it,
weaves beautifully.

— KABIR | Bijak

The Weaver

Dreams pour in through the veil of night
waiting to be woven into garments of guidance —

woolen warps of gnarled grief
silken wefts of self-compassion

and even though robes of great wisdom
embody the necessity of their destruction
I weave

and even though it is not possible to hold
'the black pearl that lies hidden under the jaws
of the deep-sea dragon' *

I embellish them
with prayer beads from Benares

weaving together dreams, consciousness,
and the Great Mystery, I become balanced
even light-hearted

*Glossary

Musings under the Snow Sky

Watching the female cardinal eating her breakfast of sunflower seeds and suet, my thoughts drift to the garden's sunflowers and spring bulbs hidden beneath the frost-kissed earth.

Perhaps they are day-dreaming too, or being dreamed; softly snoring and whistling in gentle rhythm with the deep breaths of slumbering bears in the Far North. And if they are, isn't it the same dream that we are all dreaming, the one that tugs at the heartstrings of Life?

Spring Is Coming I Know

Atop a fallen snow branch
beneath the old Japanese pine
a bright orange breast turns
towards the early morning light

spring

*"We are each sailing out on a voyage of discovery,
guided each by a private chart, of which there is no duplicate.
The world is all gates, all opportunities."*

— EMERSON | Letters and Social Aims

Perigee Tide
(haiku)

moon glories billow
full sail at dawn's early chop
on perigee tide

Blackberry Spring
(haiku)

blue-grey cloud covers

snowfield of standing stallions

ripe mango sunset

The Big Thaw

Ice melts

slush slumps

dwindles

springs rise,

as donkeys drink

from the edge

of the farm pond

once again

Before long

horses will be turned out

to frolic on fields

  that fall all the way

      down to the sea —

Is it just me

or do you think too

all this Beauty must be

why songbirds sing?

Before dawn

 a few brief notes —

the string section warming up

for Nature's Symphony

Band of Burros
(haiku)

band of brown burros

tall ears lit by setting sun

Munch! sea-swept oats

A Living Sanctuary

It's often hard to tell the difference
between buds on the old pink dogwood
that leans into spring and cardinals who perch

as faded birdhouses —
barn red   cerulean blue   goldenrod yellow
are claimed by returning homesteaders

Such a simple place
sewn with water seeds and love
is become a living sanctuary
of transformation

from one season of life into another

In the Night Garden
(haiku)

scent of wild jasmine

fleeting song of nightingale

awakens my heart

Lovers don't finally meet somewhere.
They're in each other all along.

Do you pay regular visits to yourself?

— RUMI

Talking to Myself in the Night

You, who are so good at listening,
    are you listening to me?

How else will you know I long
to dance across the high desert sky
float upon the ocean's blue breasts
dig my toes into the sands of childhood
    once again?

You, who are so good at grieving,
    are you grieving for me?

How else will you know I long
to lie down upon this Holy Earth
    to be held in her embrace
gaze at the Moon until I see one reflection
walk towards the horizon hand-in-hand?

You, who are so good at loving,
    are you loving me?

How else will you know I long
to open our heart and look at love through love,
so that we may find the peace that saves us?

*When the Soul lies down in that grass
the world is too full to talk about.*

The Dawn has secrets to tell. Don't go back to sleep.
—RUMI: "A Great Wagon"

Lying Down upon the Green

Spring is a fine time
to leave everything behind
and go outside to lie down
upon the green —

to softly gaze at the empty sky
run your fingers through
the sweet-smelling freshness

and if a dragonfly hovers
and later returns, as if to say,
"Hello, isn't the sky a fine cloudless blue?"

you, too, will understand
one of many secrets
of lying down upon the green

summer

*Live in the sunshine, swim the sea,
drink the wild air's salubrity.*

— EMERSON | "Merlin's Song"

Elephant Rock

When I was eight,
always barefoot and in a bathing suit,
I swam by myself to Elephant Rock

but my triumph was short-lived
when the tide's sudden turn
tossed me backwards into the sea

and against the rock's sharp
barnacles again and again,
until the kindness of a stranger's hand

Today there are warning signs
against swimming to Elephant Rock
but when I was eight,

always barefoot and in a bathing suit,
I learned about the importance of kindness
and how to tell time by the tides

Beach Walk Surprise
(haiku)

gleaming bright blue claw
orangutan orange saw-toothed tip
reaching for the Moon

Ocean Of Wisdom *

I once leapt over the canyon of life
back and forth   back and forth

gathering courage to dive
down and down and down
into the ocean of grief that runs through it

gathering courage to keen
tossing and turning and tumbling
into its fierce undertows of loss

and gathering courage to rise
floating and bobbing and swaying
upon its waves of wisdom and grace

*Dalai Lama: *Dalai* meaning Ocean and *Lama* meaning Wisdom

The Dance

Last night on the high tide
under the full August moon
an auburn sea blanket —

sargassum sea curls shiny serpentine kelp
wine-black berries filled with nature's breath

covered the sleeping sand

Today the beach is barren of bathers
but I walk anyway
hugging the high-water mark

where the sand is as smooth as silk
until I reach a cluster of sun-crisped sea fans
flung beneath blossoming beach roses

as if in a dance of wild abandon
under the full moon —

After all, isn't everything a Dance?

millennia of sea blankets
cradling our ancient arthropod ancestors
carried by currents from the cold Siberian Sea
to the warm, shoreless Sargasso

and the Farm Coast —
baby horseshoe crabs
(our only surviving sea fossil)
small turtles shrimp crabs
juvenile fish   endangered eels

An abundance of life
Manifesting and Non-Manifesting *
according to The Dance

Glossary

Sandpipers

all of a wing
timelessly drifting
over the deep

The Other Shore

Lying in the shallows
is the body of a small fish
freshly gutted by gulls

its Spirit already
Gone, Gone, Gone
Way Over to the Other Shore *

where white cranes float
on luminous clouds and nothing
is born, or dies

* *Glossary*

On Stellwagen Bank

We've come to see Baleen whales
feeding before migration when one
swims close alongside our boat

and stares until I recognize my wild self
covered in roses of bleached barnacles
crisscrossed by scars

before she returns to her pod's
sinuous risings in curves
surging surging surging forward

relentlessly diving for sand lace,
surfacing in whooshing white clouds —

but now one is speeding up
along the surface and launching
her enormous body
into a spinning breach against the hazy sky

smashing sideways down through
the open-palms of bright sea sprays,
to fly in unbounded freedom

tail flukes begin pounding the sea
with powerful blows
soaking us in cold salty wetness

and we are shouting for joy
at being so close to their immensity —

as if in a baptism of belonging
to this world

as the pod turns toward the horizon
dives beneath the great fire

we are diving too, inward,
into the great Thunderous Silence *

*Glossary

Summer Sunset
(haiku)

striped beach towels drying
pink elephant clouds roaming
a rosehip-hued sky

Black Swallowtail

Black swallowtail's disappearance
inside a fresh peach daylily
seems beauty enough for a morning

until she emerges fluttering
her dark wings rimmed with golden galaxies

to floats above wild blue phlox
rogue milkweed and blazing stars
in an unfettered sense of timelessness —

"Slow down", she seems to be saying,

"Seek the sweet nectars of life,
gather memories that nourish Soul"

Red-Winged Blackbird

On early morning marsh walks
red-winged blackbird greets me
in his fancy epaulets

as protector of the marshlands he sings
from tall-tipped cattails that bend
beneath his mid-toned melodies

followed by a long low rattling
like the ones of ancient healers

shaking off fears before prayer,
and time and space for experience
of eternity here and now

Amrita in the Garden *

After the rain honeybees hear
the invitational calls of foxgloves

play hide and seek inside their pink petals
of mysterious hieroglyphics

sip the sweet nectar of immortality
hidden in their hearts

*Glossary

Memories Blossomed

The Old Vintner's Daughter

Memories, yes

tastes of summer's sun
in the blackberries grapes plums
grown on the vineyard of my childhood

where I first learned to dream
with the rumbles of the sea

Memories, yes

scents of licorice tobacco coriander
cacophonies of bold merchants bartering
inside high walls of Morocco's casbahs

Memories, yes

stolen kisses under the moonlight
in Tuscan vineyards old neighborhoods
in Manhattan and the Farm Coast,
where I returned to marry my true love

Memories, yes

my rich harvest of life held
in well-seasoned barrels of sessile oak
coopered from ancient woodlands
of fairy tales I read to my grandchildren

Memories, yes

floating sinking touching fermenting
into an ever-deepening alchemy of love —

a love the color of an aged vermillion vinum,
a love the color of my Soul,
as The Old Vintner's Daughter

Permanent collection of contemporary poetry at Poets House, NYC

Their Old-Fashioned Tango

All my father wanted
was to meet us where
we dwelled in our hearts,
to shine a bright light upon
our lives, and so he did

All my mother wanted
was to cherish this man
she chose above all others,
to be his partner in life
and raise a family, and so she did

As a child I remember
watching them cook breakfast,
coffee brewing bacon-and-eggs
      sizzling
and their old-fashioned tango —

close, but not crowding
reaching, but not over
and how they did shine

Everything Tastes Better with Lemons

It wasn't until her nineties that my mother
told me of the deep affection she and my father
shared all of their married life —

at first, we giggled like schoolgirls but later on
I got to thinking of many ways their affection
showed up in our everyday lives . . .

On cold winter days, dipping our spoons
into bowls of homemade black bean soup,
with bright yellow circles of lemons on top

Saturday afternoons coming home
to find them holding hands and listening
to Grand Canyon Suite or other albums

Sunday afternoon family drives
into the deep woods in search
of another wildflower for their garden

One Last Cup of Love

My father woke early and he woke happy

his songs sweeping down the upstairs hallway

where I, as a teenager, pulled my covers up

higher over my head before meeting his happiness

but what I wouldn't give now

to open my eyes even if slowly,

to sing along even if softly,

to see him take hold of my mother's hand

so that the three of us,

trilling and twirling and swirling

could dance down the back stairs

and into our old kitchen,

for one last cup of love

Already Broken
(haiku)

the broken blue vase

shattered my last illusion

of separation

The Shell Seeker

Most summer mornings
I can be seen watching white spindrifts surf
blue-green violet waves over distant oyster beds

as tiny ghost crabs are breathing blowholes
beneath my feet in rhythm with the tides

I always search for smooth stones,
the ones with lifelines for luck, and a jingle shell —

pale-yellows   apricot-oranges   dawn grays

for once I was told by a very wise woman
I'd find a jingle on every beach to remember her by
and that's still true

Her Ladies Desk

I inherited my mother's ladies desk
with the spiny pink oyster shell
that sits on top ever since her trip to Bali

where she was greeted by Spirit Dancers
and "All the children were beautiful"

It's a small desk for writing letters by hand
with nooks and crannies for notes
and several secret compartments —

I like to keep its lid locked
see its inlay of golden flowers
spread upon our field of burnished love
that keeps our secrets safe

*Children imitating cormorants
are more delightful
than cormorants*

—ISSA

*We find delight in the beauty and happiness
of children that makes the heart
too big for the body.*

—**EMERSON** | The Conduct of Life

Little Blue Kisses

The tall blueberry bushes
planted by the farmer who built our home
still stand by the old stonewall

In spring, as I untangle them
from the wild vines in our neighbor's field
I think of him, and I wonder if he did too

In summer, as I pick plump blueberries
in dented silver buckets left behind in the shed,

reach for the rolling pin left behind in the pantry,
I wonder if the farmer did too

or did he have a wife who reached and loved
to bake blueberry pies as much as I do?

as the dark juice stains my fingers
runs down my grandchildren's chins
paints our smiles

I wonder if the farmer and his wife
(if he had a wife)
had children and grandchildren —

because if they did, I hope they ate warm wedges
of blueberry pie on hot August afternoons,
with a dollop of vanilla ice cream on top

and I hope they loved
little blue kisses as much as I do

Native Americans

A book of poems about the Farm Coast of southeastern New England would not be complete without honoring our legacy of the Mashpee Wampanoag Tribe, or their poetic language.

Migrating from Martha's Vineyard and Nantucket over 10,000 years ago, the name Wampanoag is said to translate to *People of the Dawn* or *People of the First Light*, as the first to see the sun rise.

Those who settled on the Farm Coast called themselves the Sakonnets, which is said to mean *Haunt of the Wild Black Goose*.

Askawonks , Sachem of the Sakonnets

The following is an ekphrastic poem inspired by Nancy Vibrala's mixed media collage titled "Creek's Movement" of an imagined early life of Askawonks, the Sakonnet tribe's first female sachem.

Askawonks is primarily remembered for being the first sachem to sign a peace treaty with the pilgrims in 1621, and in the late nineteenth century, she was honored with an engraved boulder in Little Compton's Wilbur Wood:

> "In memory of Awashonks,
> Queen of Sogkonate
> &
> friend of the white man."

Under the Moon of Falling Leaves

When nights grow old and days fill with wonder
Sky Bird White Owl journeys to the hunting grounds
of her ancestors, *People of the Dawn*

where Grandmother Medicine Woman showed her
how to carve a sacred flute from branch of cedar —
replace its soft red heart with breath of her own

Sky Bird White Owl journeys to give thanks
to Great Earth Mother for her one continuous
timeless being with an offering
of simah smoke on water

as she listens to Creek's Song flow over and around
smoothed stones on her path to the sea
she remembers Creek's message,
follow the Path of Peace

as she listens to the low hum of Tree Roots
healing the weakest among them
she remembers the rhythms of drumming circles
rising in Oneness

Under the Moon of Falling Leaves
Sky Bird White Owl kneels to play sacred flute songs
of Whale and Seal that the four-legged remember
their brothers and sisters of the Sea —
the one who is always calling her home

Permanent collection of contemporary poetry at Poets House, NYC

The Sioux Nation at Standing Rock

The following trilogy was written in support of Water Protectors at Standing Rock who were protesting an oil pipeline on their reservation. Their concerns were the safety of their drinking water, loss of sacred ancestral burial grounds, and its violation of the 1851 Treaty of Fort Laramie, which set aside this land for the sole use of the Sioux Nation.

"RayRay Riggin took a truckload of supplies to Standing Rock last week and your poems have reached Oceti Sakowin Camp."
— Elaine Mansfield, Award-Winning Author

"Your poems are being read at nightly campfires, where there is always poetry and drumming. We are very grateful for your support."
— RayRay Riggin, Water Protector Activist

Soul Remembering

I dreamed of my shadow lying supine
across a high mountaintop under a full moon

Face pressed to the night sky
Spirit one with omens of wolves owls buffalo
Soul remembering ancient wisdom —

"Hold strong to what you know is true"
and I needed to say something

For Land Beautiful beyond Description

Words fall from the night sky

graze upon snow-covered Black Hills

gallop on painted steeds across Great Plains

sing up the waters of the Upper Missouri

pray at the burial grounds near Lake Oahe

Words like Hallelujah Unity and Redemption

shine their light upon the broken treaty

for "Land beautiful beyond description" *

shine their light upon the Souls of Soldiers

who kneel to ask forgiveness for the deaths

of Chief Sitting Bull and all Native Souls

   embattled since Custer's Last Stand

shine their light upon the Souls of Soldiers

who kneel to ask forgiveness for taking

Native land   Native language   Native children

Where do words like these come from

Words like Hallelujah Unity and Redemption

and may they linger long and bring courage

    for the long winter ahead

May they rise with the morning sun

shine upon freshly stripped lodge poles

grace the spindrifts of white smoke from

    cooking fires and children's breaths

Words like Hallelujah Unity and Redemption

*Tribal land as described by Congress in the Fort Laramie Treaty of 1851

Permanent Collection of Contemporary Poetry at Poets House NYC

Resilience

Even though tipi ribs stand frozen in ice

Moon still follows her sky path towards Spring

White Owl still flies with the wisdom of Turtle Island

Mothers still gather their children in fading light

Grandmothers still chant for the seventh generation

A Medicine Woman still lifts her sacred flute in prayer

Even though tipi ribs stand frozen in ice

The Hopi

Old Orabi is the Hopi name for their village on top of Third Mesa in Arizona, and it is the oldest continuously inhabited community in the United States, dating from before 1100 AD.

The Hopi call themselves *Hopituh Shi nu mu*, meaning the Peaceful People, and like many tribes their ancestry is based upon matrilineal lines.

Old Orabi

East of the big canyon at Four Corners Trading Post
I ask for directions to Third Mesa

but as I drive up the long hard-packed dirt road
I'm met with the warning sounds of gunshots —

backing down, I meet a sheep herder returning from
the morning in the grasslands with his herd
and he offers to ride with me

as we pass their cemetery
filled with plastic flowers   mirrors and tinfoil
"to ward off evil spirits" the gunshots fall silent

glancing at my camera in the backseat
he asks me not to take photographs
because "Hopi believe photographs steal Souls"

At the top of the mesa at first the village
looks empty until I turn off my car engine
and children start streaming out of flat-roofed
stone and adobe dwellings with outside ladders
leading from one level to the next

smiling and asking 'a thousand questions'
they hold tight to my arms and legs
and I am happily immobilized until

the sheep herder, who turns out to be their Chief,
invites me into his home where his wife
offers us warm piki bread and green thread tea . . .

As we move into their sitting room,
high on their otherwise bare walls,
hangs a black and white photograph —

a handsome young soldier
in full U.S. military dress uniform

"Our only son" the Chief says softly
as our eyes meet in his grief

and my deepened understanding
of his tribe's perdurable persistence to protect
their right to live in accordance with their ancient,
sacred covenant —

as *Hopituh Shi-nu-mu,*
the Peaceful People

Glossary

On Allens Pond: ***Finger pointing Towards the Moon*** refers to the Dharma teaching that the Moon symbolizes eternal truth, nature, and enlightenment. Yet it is only a hint along the way because enlightenment cannot be told, only indicated.

> *Enlightenment is like the moon reflected on the water.*
> *The Moon does not get wet nor is the water broken.*
> —**Dōgen** (1200-1253)

The Sound of No Sound: ***No-Being and No Non-Being*** is a phrase Thich Nhat Hạnh added to Buddhism's sacred chant, the Heart Sutra, in September 2014. He believed it is what the Buddha most wanted to convey and is key to end suffering. When his translation was completed at 3 a.m., a ray of moonlight illuminated his text, a synchronistic sign of this enduring truth.

Jewel of the Forest Wisdom: The title refers to the Thai Forest tradition of Theravāda Buddhism, and its history of revering trees, since 500 BC. It is believed that the Buddha was born under a Sal (sacred fig) tree and entered Nirvana under grove of flowering Sals.

Moon in a dewdrop is a line from Dōgen's *Genjōkōan*, circa 1233, to convey the awe that even though its light is wide and great, the whole moon and the entire sky are reflected in a single dewdrop as a result of the moon's vastness and a dewdrop's limitlessness. The moon's reflection in dew is also a metaphor for enlightenment, the moon being enlightenment and the dewdrop a person.

The Weaver: ***The black pearl that lies hidden under the jaws of the deep-sea dragon*** reflects the difficulty of attaining enlightenment.

A Small Fish: ***Gone, gone way over to the other shore*** is a line from Buddhism's sacred Heart Sutra chant and represents a life's completed transition from this world. Other translations include: "Enlightened, so be it."

The Dance: ***Life manifesting and non-manifesting*** refers to our eternal selves, and whether we are in this world in physical bodies, or what is often called the Other World, or the non-physical realm.

On Stellwagen Bank: ***The Thunderous Silence.*** Near the end of his life, Buddha told his followers he had not said anything in his teachings to encourage them to get caught by words or ideas. Thich Nhat Hạnh called this "the roar of a great lion, the thundering silence of Buddha".

Amrita in the Garden: In Hinduism, the moon is considered to be a vessel of Amrita, the sacred water that sustains all living creatures and brings immortality.

The following poems were previously published:

Pathfinder Magazine

"Come Lie With Me"
"Talking to Myself in the Night"
   (titled "Souls Longing for Itself")
"Ocean of Wisdom"
   (titled "I Once Leapt")

Wickford Poetry & Art *

"Lowly Listening"
"The Old Vintner's Daughter"
"For Land Beautiful Beyond Description"
"Under the Moon of Falling Leaves"

* These, and other poems that are not in this book, are part of the permanent collection of contemporary poetry at Poet's House, New York City.

Acknowledgments

A deep bow to the late poet and professor Thomas Fitzsimmons, translator of ancient haiku and author of more than sixty books, including his own poetry and *Asian Poetry in Translation*, for his encouragement and years of sharing our poems. Also, to award-winning independent author Elaine Mansfield, and poet, song writer, and musician Edward Keneski for our enduring friendships and creative support.

Thank you to Tuesdays at Ten, led by Grace Farrell, co-founder of Carolina Fiber and Fiction Center, who first read and critiqued some of these poems, and to The Poetry Salon, hosted by Lisa Starr, Rhode Island's Poet Laureate Emerita, for workshops and public readings. I also want to thank Patricia Chaffee, award-winning journalist and poetry editor of Pathfinder Magazine, for first publishing my poems, and Ann Ryden, juror at Wickford Art Gallery, for selecting my poems for their Poetry & Art Exhibitions and publishing books that are now in the permanent collection at Poets House in New York City.

My deepest gratitude is to my family for their unconditional love. To my daughter, Sarah Kate, for her caring and perceptive insights, in addition to designing the press logo with our chocolate field lab; to my son, Benjamin, for his thoughtful listening and perspectives; and to my husband, Mark, for our love, our devotion to family, and our shared spiritual journey.

About the Author

Sarah Ragsdale grew up on the Farm Coast of southeastern New England. In college, she spent a semester in Florence, Italy, and returned after graduating to volunteer with the restoration of flood-damaged art at the Uffizi Gallery. During that time, she taught English as a Second Language at the American Institute, traveled throughout Italy, and visited Greece, Sardinia, Ceuta, Morocco, Lisbon, Paris, and London.

She earned her MA in Linguistics and Education from Teachers College, Columbia University, with post-graduate studies in Linguistics and at Brown University's Bilingual Institute. She then taught Advanced English to foreign Chiefs of Staff at the United Nations, and was on staff at Bank Street College of Education for the development of bilingual education. She lives with her husband in South Country, Rhode Island where she enjoys spending time with family, friends, and writing with local groups. In 2023, she founded Rudd Rambles Press in honor of her mother's maiden name and their love of poetry and travel.

www.ruddrambles.com

Rudd Rambles Press is an independent publisher located in South County, Rhode Island with a mission to kindle a deeper interconnectedness with all life through poetry for adults and stories for children.

In 2023, *Lucy's Lopsided Web*, was published with lines from well-known nature poems and "This World", by Pulitzer Prize winning poet Mary Oliver, on the end page by permission of her literary agency and estate.

For additional information and to contact us, please visit our website at www.ruddrambles.com.

www.ingramcontent.com/pod-product-compliance
Lightning Source LLC
Chambersburg PA
CBHW031258290426
44109CB00012B/631